SONG OF SONGS
FROM START2FINISH

MICHAEL WHITWORTH

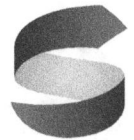

© 2025 by Start2Finish

All rights reserved. No part of this publication may be reproduced, stored in a retrieval system, or transmitted in any form or by any means without the prior written permission of the author. The only exception is brief quotations in printed reviews.

ISBN 978-1-944704-23-0

Published by Start2Finish
Bend, Oregon 97702
start2finish.org

Printed in the United States of America

Unless otherwise noted, all Scripture quotations are from The Holy Bible, English Standard Version®, copyright © 2001 by Crossway Bibles, a publishing ministry of Good News Publishers. Used by permission. All rights reserved.

Cover Design: Evangela Creative

CONTENTS

1.	The Lovers Presented	5
2.	Springtime in Palestine	13
3.	The Terrors of the Night	21
4.	A Man Enraptured	29
5.	The Lovers Entranced	37
6.	The Dance of Delights	45
7.	Love Strong As Death	53

1

THE LOVERS PRESENTED

SONG OF SONGS 1

Objective: To celebrate the holiness of romantic love expressed through purity, humility, and covenant faithfulness.

INTRODUCTION

On their fiftieth wedding anniversary, an elderly husband stood up at the reception to give a toast. With a shaky hand and tearful smile, he raised his glass and said, "After all these years, I still get butterflies when she walks into the room." The guests laughed softly, but his wife's eyes filled with tears. That single sentence captured the beauty of enduring love—passion preserved by faithfulness.

The Song of Songs celebrates that kind of love. It is not about infatuation or fleeting attraction but the joy of affection sanctified by covenant. From the first verse, the poem invites readers into the beauty of intimacy as God intended it—where purity and passion coexist. The opening chapter introduces the lovers, revealing how admiration, humility, and commitment form the foundation of true romance. Here we learn that godly love is not embarrassed by desire, and that holiness can dwell joyfully within human affection.

EXAMINATION

The song of songs (1:1)

The book opens with a simple but majestic title: "The Song of Songs, which is Solomon's." The repetition signals superlative excellence—this is the finest of all songs. In a world full of lament and war poetry, here is a poem of love and joy. The Bible begins with a marriage in Eden and ends with a wedding feast in Revelation, and between them stands this "greatest song," sanctifying human affection as God intended.

Attributing the song to Solomon links it to Israel's golden age of wisdom and prosperity. He "spoke 3,000 proverbs, and his songs were 1,005" (1 Kgs. 4:32). Yet this song surpasses the rest because it celebrates covenant love rooted in wisdom and fidelity, not in the fleeting pleasures that later ensnared Solomon. The mention of his name may indicate authorship, dedication, or royal setting, but the theology remains clear: love's beauty is a divine creation, and when expressed within covenant faithfulness, it reflects heaven's own harmony.

For centuries, Jewish and Christian interpreters have wrestled with the Song's place in Scripture. Some allegorized it as the love between God and Israel or Christ and the church. Others, reading more literally, recognized its power to sanctify marital affection. The best reading sees both realities intertwined—earthly love as a mirror of divine love. God created passion, companionship, and desire; therefore, they are good when governed by holiness.

The bride's longing (1:2-4)

The first voice we hear is the woman's, not the man's. In a patriarchal world, this is remarkable. Scripture gives the bride the opening lines of love's greatest song, validating the woman's voice and desire. "Let him kiss me with the kisses of his mouth! For your love is better than wine." The Hebrew word for "love" (*dodim*) often refers to physical affection, yet here it carries emotional depth—an intimacy born of devotion, not lust.

Wine in ancient Israel symbolized joy and celebration. Her comparison means that her beloved's love brings a delight surpassing life's finest pleasures. The fragrance of his oils and his "name poured out" (1:3) convey the reputation of his character. A godly man's virtue is as pleasing as perfume; his integrity draws others to him. Thus, desire and moral beauty intertwine. True love rests not only on attraction but also on character.

The chorus of "the virgins" (1:3–4) functions like a Greek chorus, offering communal affirmation. Their exclamation—"We will exult and rejoice in you"—reminds readers that love is not shameful. Righteous affection can be celebrated publicly, within the covenant community, because it honors God's design. In a culture where love is often trivialized or hidden in shame, the Song restores dignity to passion disciplined by purity.

The bride's humility and insecurity (1:5–7)

"I am very dark, but lovely." The woman acknowledges her natural beauty while recognizing her humble background. Her complexion, darkened by the sun, contrasts with courtly ideals of pale skin. She has worked outdoors, "the sun has looked upon me." Her brothers forced her to keep the vineyards, so she "did not keep" her own—an image of neglected self-care under harsh circumstances. Yet she does not despise herself. She is both aware of imperfection and confident in her worth.

Her humility is instructive. In marriage, insecurity can distort intimacy; but this woman models self-acceptance rooted in being loved. She does not seek to change her appearance to earn affection—she already has it. She then expresses longing to be near her beloved: "Tell me, you whom my soul loves, where you pasture your flock." She desires connection, not conquest. Love's goal is presence, not possession.

Her language of shepherd and flock may have symbolic layers. The man may literally be a shepherd, or "shepherd" may serve as a pastoral metaphor for one who leads with care and tenderness. Either way, she rejects the company of "those who veil themselves"—a possible reference to immodest or unfaithful women. The bride's request shows both passion and purity: she wants intimacy without compromising holiness.

The king's praise (1:8–11)

The man responds with admiration, guiding her to the pastures: "If you do not know, O most beautiful among women, follow in the tracks of the flock." His words reassure and honor her. He calls her "most beautiful," affirming her worth rather than correcting her insecurity. Love speaks life. His imagery—"a mare among Pharaoh's chariots"—sounds odd to modern ears but carried strong romantic connotations in the ancient world. Stallions pulled Pharaoh's chariots; introducing a mare among them would captivate and distract every eye. His point: her presence commands attention; her grace overwhelms.

He continues, "Your cheeks are lovely with ornaments, your neck with strings of jewels." Whether she wears literal jewelry or not, his words adorn her with dignity. Verse 11, perhaps voiced by companions, adds, "We will make for you ornaments of gold." Love delights in giving, not taking. Where lust objectifies, love beautifies. This exchange models verbal affection within marriage—words that affirm, not diminish. Proverbs 31:28 says, "Her husband praises her." The Song exemplifies that truth.

The lovers' mutual delight (1:12–14)

As the dialogue continues, the woman describes her beloved's nearness: "While the king was on his couch, my nard gave forth its fragrance." Her perfume represents the allure of love, but the focus is relational. She calls him "a sachet of myrrh that lies between my breasts" and "a cluster of henna blossoms in the vineyards of En-gedi." These metaphors express continual delight and remembrance. In the ancient world, myrrh was worn close to the heart to release fragrance throughout the day. Her beloved's presence fills her life with sweetness and comfort.

En-gedi, an oasis near the Dead Sea, was lush and fragrant—a fitting symbol of refreshment amid arid surroundings. Marriage can be that oasis: a refuge of joy and renewal amid life's wilderness. The text invites Christians to cultivate such delight—not through self-indulgence, but through faithful devotion that nurtures joy and tenderness.

The man's praise renewed (1:15)

The man's voice returns: "Behold, you are beautiful, my love; behold, you are beautiful; your eyes are doves." Repetition reinforces sincerity. Doves symbolize purity, gentleness, and loyalty. In the ancient Near East, doves also represented peace and fertility—qualities that fit this moment of harmony. His words convey both admiration and safety. The eyes are windows of the soul, and he delights in what he sees within her.

In a world where beauty is often reduced to surface appearance, this verse reminds Christians that true attraction includes moral and emotional depth. Husbands and wives are called to behold—not merely glance at—each other with wonder renewed daily.

The bride's response and shared home (1:16–17)

She answers joyfully: "Behold, you are beautiful, my beloved, truly delightful." Their mutual admiration underscores equality within covenant love. Both give and receive affirmation. Their "couch is green," perhaps meaning grassy fields or the freshness of springtime. Nature joins in their song, suggesting that creation itself rejoices in godly love. "The beams of our house are cedar, our rafters are pine." Whether literal or symbolic, this imagery portrays strength, stability, and fragrance—qualities of enduring love.

Cedar, used in temple construction, hints that their union partakes of holiness. Their relationship, like a temple, is a dwelling place of joy and covenant faithfulness. The poet thus closes the first movement of the Song with a picture of harmony—two voices, equally heard, rejoicing in mutual delight.

The theology of love

Song of Songs 1 invites readers to revere love as sacred. It affirms desire without shame and affection without impurity. The woman's voice shows that God values both partners' dignity; the man's praise shows that strength and tenderness coexist. Together they model Genesis 2:24—"The two shall become one flesh." This is not a utilitarian union but a joyful partnership grounded in mutual respect.

In the church, this vision of marriage corrects distortions both ancient and modern. Against asceticism, it teaches that bodily affection is good; against hedonism, it insists that love thrives only in faithfulness. The same God who designed intimacy also defined its boundaries. Thus, every married couple who delights in one another within covenant faith mirrors the Creator's wisdom.

The first chapter, then, is not merely romantic poetry—it is moral theology in verse. It presents love as something to be celebrated, cultivated, and guarded. In a culture where desire is often detached from commitment, the Song reminds us that holiness and happiness meet in the garden of covenant love.

APPLICATION

1. God designed love to be both passionate and pure

The Song opens with vivid imagery of desire, yet it never descends into vulgarity. Love as God intended it involves deep affection without moral compromise. In a culture that separates passion from purity, this chapter teaches that holiness enhances desire rather than suppressing it. A Christian marriage should never be cold or transactional. Husbands and wives are invited to delight in one another physically and emotionally within the safe boundaries of covenant faithfulness. This kind of passion is not sinful—it is sacred. God delights when married couples rejoice in his good design. Genuine intimacy flows from commitment, trust, and godliness, not from indulgence.

2. Verbal affirmation strengthens the bond of marriage

The lovers' dialogue is filled with praise, admiration, and gratitude. They build one another up through kind words. The man repeatedly calls his bride "beautiful"; she responds in kind. This reminds Christians that affection must be expressed, not assumed. Words of affirmation breathe life into relationships; silence can suffocate love. A husband who speaks encouragement reflects Christ's tenderness toward the church. A wife who honors her husband's character demonstrates reverence and respect. Mutual affirmation is not flattery—it is ministry. Our words can either wound or heal, and when spoken in love, they nurture joy and stability within marriage. Godly speech is one of the most powerful ways couples can glorify God in their relationship.

3. True beauty is rooted in character, not appearance.

The bride confesses her insecurity about her darkened skin, yet her beloved treasures her as "most beautiful among women." This exchange reveals the difference between worldly and godly beauty. Outer charm fades, but inner grace endures (Prov. 31:30). The Song of Songs elevates beauty grounded in humility, faithfulness, and virtue. Christians must reject the world's shallow ideals that prize youth and perfection over godliness. The beauty that lasts is the beauty of the heart—a life shaped by integrity, gentleness, and joy. When believers cultivate these virtues, their relationships deepen and their witness strengthens. Every marriage grows richer when partners see one another as God does—beloved, valuable, and made in his image.

4. Covenant love reflects the heart of God

The joy between the bride and groom mirrors divine affection. Though this poem celebrates human marriage, it also whispers of the greater love that God has for his people. His love is faithful, tender, and unending. Christian marriages become living parables of that love. When husbands and wives pursue faithfulness, forgiveness, and sacrifice, they proclaim the gospel in daily life. Marriage is not merely about companionship—it is about covenant. The same God who bound Israel to himself now calls Christians to reflect that steadfast love in their homes. To love faithfully is to participate in the divine story. Our relationships, purified by grace, point others to the One whose love never fails.

CONCLUSION

The opening chapter of the Song of Songs reminds believers that love is both divine and human, both tender and strong. It affirms that God is not embarrassed by affection when it is pure and covenantal. In the voices of the bride and groom, we hear mutual admiration, humility, and joy—elements that sustain lifelong faithfulness. Their relationship is not built on perfection but on devotion and delight. When Christians embrace God's design for love, they rediscover that marriage is not a mere contract but a covenant of grace. Every home shaped by this truth becomes a small reflection of the steadfast love of the Lord.

REFLECTION

1. What does this chapter reveal about God's view of romantic love and desire?

2. How does the woman's voice at the beginning of the Song challenge cultural expectations about gender and intimacy?

3. Why is it significant that the bride and groom both praise one another openly?

4. In what ways does humility make a person more attractive spiritually and emotionally?

5. How can married Christians keep affection and admiration alive over the years?

6. What does this passage teach about the holiness of love within God's design?

DISCUSSION

1. How can churches better affirm marriage as both sacred and joyful?

2. What practical ways can couples use words to build one another up?

3. How does the Song of Songs correct both lustful and prudish distortions of love?

4. What are some modern "vineyards" that distract believers from nurturing their relationships?

5. How does mutual admiration in marriage reflect the gospel?

6. What can this chapter teach single Christians about preparing for godly love?

2

SPRINGTIME IN PALESTINE

SONG OF SONGS 2

Objective: To celebrate love's renewal as a divine gift that flourishes through purity, patience, and protection.

INTRODUCTION

After a long and bitter winter, there's something almost sacred about the first signs of spring—the scent of rain-soaked soil, the budding of trees, the song of a meadowlark cutting through the quiet. Each signal whispers that life has returned. What was dormant begins to bloom again.

The second chapter of the Song of Songs captures that same feeling. It is a celebration of renewal—love awakened, confidence restored, and joy shared. The bride and groom delight in one another with fresh wonder, as if love itself has stepped into a new season. The imagery of springtime in Palestine—flowers, doves, and ripening fruit—mirrors the renewal of affection between them. Through their voices, we learn that love, like faith, requires tending and patience. When nurtured in purity and faithfulness, love blossoms into something both beautiful and enduring—a garden where God's design flourishes.

EXAMINATION

The beauty of love renewed (2:1-7)

The second song begins in the language of spring. The woman speaks: "I am a rose of Sharon, a lily of the valleys." Her words are not boastful but humble. The rose and lily were common flowers in Israel—delicate, beautiful, yet ordinary. She sees herself as one among many, not as one above all. Love has given her confidence, but not pride.

Her beloved immediately answers: "As a lily among brambles, so is my love among the young women." What she sees as ordinary, he sees as incomparable. His reply transforms her self-perception. Love always has that power—to take what feels plain and reveal its worth. He compares her purity to a lily and the rest of the world to thorns. In his eyes, she stands out for her gentleness, grace, and faithfulness.

The woman answers in kind: "As an apple tree among the trees of the forest, so is my beloved among the young men." The apple tree was a symbol of shade and nourishment in a dry climate. She delights to sit under his shadow and taste his fruit—a poetic way of saying that she finds security, pleasure, and refreshment in his presence. Where others are barren, he gives life.

"He brought me to the banqueting house, and his banner over me was love." The phrase "banqueting house" may literally mean "house of wine," a place of feasting and joy. The "banner" suggests public declaration, as in a military or royal procession. His love is not hidden; it is proudly displayed. She is not a secret affair or a passing fancy. She is cherished openly and honored completely.

The passage continues, "Sustain me with raisins; refresh me with apples, for I am sick with love." Ancient readers would have understood "sick with love" not as weakness but as overwhelmed emotion—intense longing for closeness. Her heart can hardly contain the joy and anticipation that love brings. "His left hand is under my head, and his right hand embraces me." The scene describes affection expressed with tenderness, not lust. Their love is passionate but restrained, affectionate yet pure.

Then comes the refrain that will appear several times in the Song: "I adjure you, O daughters of Jerusalem… that you not stir up or awaken love until it pleases." This refrain is a boundary line. The poet reminds readers that love must never be rushed or forced. Desire is a powerful gift; it must unfold in its proper time and within God's design. The lovers' affection is not a license for passion outside covenant—it is a celebration of passion within it.

The call to arise (2:8–13)

The scene shifts suddenly from the chamber to the outdoors. The woman hears her beloved's voice calling from afar: "The voice of my beloved! Behold, he comes, leaping over the mountains, bounding over the hills." The imagery captures energy and eagerness. Her beloved is not reluctant—he races to be near her. In him, strength and tenderness unite. The picture recalls a gazelle or young stag—creatures known for vitality and grace.

He calls to her through the lattice: "Arise, my love, my beautiful one, and come away." The invitation is filled with joy, not command. He urges her to share in the renewal of spring, a season symbolic of new beginnings and flourishing love. The language is lush: "For behold, the winter is past; the rain is over and gone. The flowers appear on the earth, the time of singing has come." Each image echoes a spiritual truth—love, like faith, awakens from dormancy into life.

The call continues: "The voice of the turtledove is heard in our land. The fig tree ripens its figs, and the vines are in blossom." These signs of fertility and abundance mirror the blossoming of their relationship. Their love has matured beyond longing into invitation—an open call to unity and shared delight. Springtime becomes a metaphor for the joy of covenant renewal. Just as creation sings in harmony after winter's silence, so love renews the soul after loneliness.

This poetic passage reminds readers that love, rightly nurtured, is alive. It grows, changes, and flourishes in seasons. The couple's affection is not static—it deepens and ripens. Their courtship is moving toward consummation, yet always within the framework of patience and respect. The repeated "Arise, my love" calls to every believer as well: love should awaken gratitude, not greed; joy, not selfishness.

The plea for protection (2:14–15)

In verse 14, the man's voice softens. "O my dove, in the clefts of the rock, in the crannies of the cliff, let me see your face, let me hear your voice."

Doves often hid in rock crevices for safety, a symbol of gentleness and vulnerability. He calls her out from hiding—not to expose her, but to assure her. He longs to see her and hear her, because her voice is "sweet" and her face "lovely." Here, love is not pursuit alone; it is protection. He honors her modesty, draws her out of fear, and delights in her presence.

Then comes one of the Song's most memorable lines: "Catch the foxes for us, the little foxes that spoil the vineyards, for our vineyards are in blossom." The vineyards symbolize their love, now flourishing. The "little foxes" represent threats that could ruin it—perhaps jealousy, impatience, misunderstanding, or moral temptation. In ancient Palestine, foxes would burrow among grapevines and destroy the roots. The metaphor teaches that love, even when strong, is fragile if neglected. Small compromises can corrode great affection.

Every marriage and courtship must guard against these "little foxes." Bitterness, neglect, harsh words, or selfish habits can quickly damage intimacy. The couple's appeal—"Catch the foxes for us"—shows shared responsibility. Both partners must protect the relationship. Love is not sustained by emotion alone but by vigilance and care.

The declaration of belonging (2:16–17)

The woman concludes this section with a confident confession: "My beloved is mine, and I am his; he grazes among the lilies." This mutual belonging stands at the heart of covenant love. It is not ownership in the sense of control, but mutual devotion born of commitment. Love gives itself freely and receives the other wholly. The exclusivity of this statement contrasts sharply with the world's casual view of relationships. Here, fidelity is celebrated, not constrained.

The closing lines—"Until the day breathes and the shadows flee, turn, my beloved, be like a gazelle or a young stag on cleft mountains"—echo the longing of separation and anticipation of reunion. The imagery of dawn suggests hope: their union awaits fulfillment, but it will come in the right time. Love that waits in purity grows stronger, not weaker.

The theology of renewal

This chapter captures the freshness of love as something divinely ordained. Springtime in Palestine becomes a parable for renewal in relationships and in faith. The cold rains of winter symbolize absence or struggle; the warmth of spring mirrors the return of joy. The poet weaves creation and affection into a single tapestry, reminding believers that love is part of God's good creation. It is not an intrusion into holiness but an expression of it.

Moreover, the repetition of restraint—"Do not awaken love until it pleases"—shows that genuine love honors divine timing. Lust demands; love waits. Impulse takes; covenant gives. The lovers' joy flows from patience, not passion unbridled. When desire is guided by devotion, it becomes a force for life, not destruction.

The Song also highlights mutuality. Both voices speak, both invite, both delight. The woman initiates and responds; the man leads and listens. This balance reveals the divine wisdom behind partnership. In God's design, marriage is not dominance but harmony—each blessing the other through affection, respect, and grace.

Finally, the imagery of nature reminds Christians that love is part of creation's praise. The same God who formed the fig tree and clothed the fields also formed human hearts for relationship. When love blossoms in purity and faithfulness, it joins the chorus of creation singing, "The winter is past."

APPLICATION

1. Godly love restores identity and confidence

The bride begins unsure of her beauty, but her beloved's affirmation transforms her self-image. Love that honors God always uplifts rather than degrades. In marriage, spouses should echo this pattern—speaking life into one another's insecurities. A husband's praise and a wife's encouragement are not flattery; they are grace in words. True affection reflects how God sees his people—valuable, cherished, and lovely in his sight. When Christians practice this kind of affirmation, they mirror divine compassion. Our words can become instruments of renewal, helping those we love see themselves through the lens of grace, not comparison. The Song reminds believers that the best relationships restore dignity and deepen confidence through selfless devotion.

2. Love flourishes when it follows God's timing

Twice the poet warns, "Do not awaken love until it pleases." Passion is a gift, but it is powerful. Like fire, it must be contained within the hearth of covenant. When desire precedes commitment, love's beauty is distorted. The world urges impatience, yet Scripture teaches restraint. Waiting honors God and strengthens trust. For dating Christians, this means guarding physical and emotional intimacy until marriage. For married couples, it means renewing affection in patience and tenderness, not selfish haste. God's timing is always perfect; love that submits to his wisdom is love that endures. The Song's refrain is a call to purity that protects joy, not suppresses it.

3. Lasting love must be carefully protected

The lovers' plea to "catch the little foxes" warns that even strong relationships can be undermined by small compromises. Disrespect, neglect, and unspoken resentment are subtle predators. They sneak in unnoticed and slowly erode affection. Every Christian marriage must guard its vineyard by daily tending to communication, prayer, and forgiveness. Healthy love does not happen by accident—it grows through vigilance and grace. The most enduring marriages are not the ones without conflict but the ones that confront it quickly and kindly. God calls couples to defend their bond as fiercely as they delight in it. When Christians guard love from the "little foxes," their homes become vineyards where the fruit of the Spirit can flourish.

4. Covenant love mirrors God's faithfulness

"My beloved is mine, and I am his." With that declaration, the bride expresses both intimacy and exclusivity. Their love is not a fleeting emotion but a covenant commitment. This kind of belonging reflects the relationship between Christ and the church. God's people belong to him not through coercion but through covenant grace. Christian marriages become living illustrations of that truth. Spouses who serve, forgive, and remain faithful proclaim the gospel with their lives. The love that lasts is love anchored in covenant, not convenience. When believers live out this mutual devotion, they display the steadfast love of the Lord before a watching world.

CONCLUSION

Springtime in Palestine reminds believers that love, like creation, thrives under God's care. The lovers' joy reflects not fleeting passion but faithfulness renewed. Their relationship is alive because it is guarded, pure, and grounded in commitment. The warnings about awakening love too soon and catching the little foxes teach that affection must mature under wisdom. Just as winter yields to spring, hearts that trust God's timing find renewal after seasons of weariness or distance. Love that waits, protects, and rejoices becomes a testimony of divine grace. In every marriage and friendship shaped by such care, the beauty of God's design blossoms again.

REFLECTION

1. What does this passage teach about God's design for the growth and renewal of love?

2. How does the bride's humility shape our understanding of healthy self-image in relationships?

3. Why is the refrain "Do not awaken love until it pleases" repeated so often in the Song?

4. What "little foxes" have the potential to threaten intimacy in a marriage or friendship?

5. How does creation imagery in this chapter deepen our appreciation for God's design of love?

6. In what ways can believers reflect covenant faithfulness through their own relationships?

DISCUSSION

1. How can couples nurture springtime renewal in long-term relationships?

2. What practical ways can Christians guard love from emotional or spiritual "foxes"?

3. How might this passage guide dating believers in purity and patience?

4. What does mutual admiration between the lovers reveal about God's view of equality in marriage?

5. How can churches better support healthy, faithful marriages within their communities?

6. What parallels do you see between this love poem and God's covenant love for his people?

# 3

THE TERRORS OF THE NIGHT
SONG OF SONGS 3

Objective: To learn that steadfast love perseveres through fear, guards covenant purity, and rejoices in faithful reunion.

INTRODUCTION

Not long after their wedding, a young husband was called away on military duty. His wife described those months apart as "the longest nights of my life." She would lie awake listening to the wind, clutching his last letter, longing for the sound of his return. When he finally came home, she said, "It felt like the whole world exhaled."

That sense of yearning and relief captures the emotion of Song of Songs 3. The bride dreams of losing her beloved and rises in the night to search for him. Her fear turns to joy when she finds him again and refuses to let go. The passage reminds us that even the strongest love endures seasons of absence and anxiety. Yet in every dark night, love's faithfulness becomes its greatest light. The terrors of the night cannot conquer hearts bound by covenant devotion.

EXAMINATION

Searching for love (3:1-4)

The third movement of the Song begins with longing and loss. "On my bed by night I sought him whom my soul loves; I sought him, but found him not." The gentle joy of springtime in the previous chapter gives way to the unease of separation. The woman dreams—or perhaps recalls—a night filled with absence. Her beloved is gone, and her soul aches for his presence.

The setting of the "night" suggests emotional as well as physical darkness. This is not mere loneliness; it is the dread that love once known might be lost. She rises to search the city streets, saying, "I will seek him whom my soul loves." The repetition of that phrase four times (vv. 1-4) intensifies her devotion. Her love is not casual or convenient; it compels pursuit. Even in the night, she refuses to give up.

Ancient readers often understood this as a dream sequence—an anxious vision that reveals the depth of the bride's longing. The imagery resembles that of the Psalms, where the faithful seek God in the night watches. Here, however, it is the longing of human love—a reflection of the same steadfast devotion. Her love is awake even when the world sleeps.

She encounters the watchmen patrolling the city. "Have you seen him whom my soul loves?" The watchmen symbolize order and protection, yet they cannot satisfy her longing or direct her to her beloved. True love cannot be delegated or replaced; it must be found personally. Her search continues until, at last, "I found him whom my soul loves." Relief replaces anxiety; absence yields to presence.

The joy of reunion overflows into intimacy: "I held him, and would not let him go until I had brought him into my mother's house, and into the chamber of her who conceived me." The "mother's house" was the traditional place of preparation for marriage—a symbol of security, not impropriety. The scene emphasizes her desire to anchor their love within family and covenant. The chamber she mentions is not the site of seduction but of union blessed by community and tradition. Love that is pure seeks protection, not secrecy.

This section captures a universal truth: love endures both presence and absence, delight and distress. Even the strongest relationships pass through seasons of distance—emotional, physical, or circumstantial. The bride's perseverance becomes a model for faithfulness. She does not replace her beloved or resign herself to despair; she searches until she finds him. In that persistence lies the mark of covenant love.

The refrain of restraint (3:5)

Before the next scene unfolds, the familiar refrain returns: "I adjure you, O daughters of Jerusalem, by the gazelles or the does of the field, that you not stir up or awaken love until it pleases." This repeated warning marks the end of each major scene of intimacy or emotional climax. It reminds readers that passion, though beautiful, must be governed by wisdom.

The imagery of gazelles and does invokes the natural world—creatures of grace and sensitivity easily startled by sudden movement. So too, love must not be forced. The bride's journey through longing and fulfillment underscores that love's deepest joys cannot be rushed. Every season has its purpose. Those who wait for God's timing experience not only joy but peace.

The royal procession (3:6–10)

The scene shifts dramatically from private dream to public display. The poet asks, "What is that coming up from the wilderness like columns of smoke, perfumed with myrrh and frankincense, with all the fragrant powders of a merchant?" The imagery of smoke rising from the desert signals grandeur and anticipation. A royal procession approaches—Solomon himself, borne on a litter surrounded by sixty warriors, "all of them experts in war."

The wilderness evokes Israel's past—the place of testing and transformation. Out of that barren land emerges beauty, strength, and ceremony. The bride's beloved, perhaps identified with Solomon here, comes in regal splendor. Some interpreters see this as a literal wedding procession; others read it symbolically, a poetic depiction of love's triumph. Either way, the focus is not on wealth but on honor. The bride is not an ornament of the king's power; she is the reason for his celebration.

Every detail of the scene radiates majesty. "Behold, it is the litter of Solomon. Around it are sixty mighty men, some of the mighty men of Israel, all of them wearing swords and expert in war, each with his sword at his thigh, against terror by night." The reference to "terror by night" connects this scene to the opening verses. The anxiety of the bride's night search gives way to the security of royal protection. Love that once trembled in fear now rests under the strength of covenant promise.

The litter itself—an ornate carriage—"made of the wood of Lebanon." "Its posts [are] of silver, its back of gold, its seat of purple; its interior was inlaid with love by the daughters of Jerusalem." This is one of the most striking lines in the Song. The bridal couch is literally "inlaid with love"—a poetic reminder that true beauty in marriage comes not from materials or wealth, but from affection, loyalty, and shared joy. The finery of gold and silver only symbolizes what truly adorns the union: love itself.

This description may evoke the temple imagery familiar to Israel's readers. Lebanon's cedar, silver, gold, and purple all appear in the construction of the tabernacle and temple (Exod. 26; 1 Kgs. 6–7). Just as the temple was built for the meeting of God and his people, so the wedding procession celebrates the meeting of husband and wife within covenant love. The Song thereby sanctifies the marriage bond as something holy and worthy of honor.

The crown of joy (3:11)

The section concludes with an invitation: "Go out, O daughters of Zion, and look upon King Solomon, with the crown with which his mother crowned him on the day of his wedding, on the day of the gladness of his heart." The focus now shifts to communal joy. The "daughters of Zion"—representing society at large—are called to witness the beauty and blessing of marital love.

In Israel's culture, weddings were public celebrations, not private escapes. The crowning of Solomon by his mother adds familial blessing to royal ceremony. The "day of his wedding" is "the day of the gladness of his heart." Marriage is not merely duty or alliance; it is joy. The crown symbolizes honor freely given, not demanded. Love is the glory of a man's life and the gladness of his heart.

Some scholars note that Solomon's mother, Bathsheba, had known both sorrow and redemption. Her participation in this moment enriches the symbolism: love, though it may emerge from brokenness, can be restored by grace. Joy after pain, reunion after separation—this is the rhythm of the Song and the rhythm of redeemed love.

The theology of love in darkness

This chapter portrays love not only in delight but also in difficulty. The bride's nocturnal search reflects the reality that even the truest relationships experience seasons of uncertainty. Love is tested in absence, refined in waiting, and crowned in faithfulness. The terrors of the night—loneliness, doubt, fear—are not signs that love has failed but opportunities for it to deepen.

The progression from darkness to dawn, from searching to celebration, mirrors the spiritual journey of believers. At times God seems distant, and the soul searches in the night. But those who seek him with steadfast devotion find that he has never truly left. The reunion brings greater joy than before. Similarly, in marriage, periods of separation or conflict can lead to deeper trust when both partners seek restoration with humility.

The grandeur of Solomon's procession also teaches that love thrives within covenant structure. The Song does not glorify reckless passion but ordered devotion. The security of covenant—symbolized by soldiers and the royal litter—protects love from chaos. Within that boundary, joy flourishes.

Finally, the "crown" on Solomon's head reminds us that marriage, when entered in faith, is not a burden but a blessing. It is the gladness of the heart, a divine gift worthy of reverence and celebration. Love that endures the night emerges stronger, brighter, and more beautiful at dawn.

APPLICATION

1. Faithful love endures even through seasons of absence

The bride's restless search through the night reminds believers that every relationship faces moments of distance—times when affection cools, communication falters, or circumstances separate loved ones. But covenant love does not give up when comfort disappears. It seeks, it perseveres, it prays. The woman's determination to find her beloved illustrates love that is loyal, not fleeting. Christian marriages grow stronger when spouses choose persistence over passivity, even in the dark. Faith is not the absence of longing but the decision to keep searching. When believers seek reconciliation and renewal with the same resolve as the bride, they echo God's own steadfast love—a love that never stops pursuing.

2. True love seeks covenant security, not secrecy

When the bride finds her beloved, she brings him to her mother's house—the symbol of family and covenant blessing. Love that is genuine welcomes the light of community and the approval of righteousness. The world often romanticizes secrecy, treating hidden relationships as exciting, but Scripture teaches the opposite: love flourishes in truth and transparency. For the Christian, affection and intimacy belong within the safety of marriage. God's boundaries are not barriers to joy but the walls that protect it. The bride's example reminds believers that the greatest satisfaction comes when love is rooted in purity, not passion alone.

3. Every marriage must guard against the "terrors of the night"

Solomon's royal procession surrounded by armed guards "against terror by night" symbolizes how love must be defended. Marriages and friendships face unseen threats—resentment, neglect, pride, or temptation. The night seasons of fear and fatigue can invite these enemies into the heart. Godly couples protect their covenant through prayer, honesty, and forgiveness. Spiritual vigilance is not distrust; it is devotion. The same God who commands the stars watches over our homes when we walk in faith. Just as Solomon's warriors kept watch, believers must stand guard over their hearts, resisting anything that would darken joy or destroy unity.

4. Love's ultimate victory is found in covenant joy

The chapter ends not in fear but in celebration—a royal procession crowned with gladness. The bride's anxiety gives way to rejoicing. Likewise, love anchored in faith and commitment always finds its crown in joy. Marital happiness is not achieved by avoiding hardship but by persevering through it with trust. The "day of gladness" comes to those who endure the night with grace. Every Christian marriage that survives trial becomes a living testimony of divine mercy. When spouses forgive and remain steadfast, they reflect Christ's unwavering love for his church. God's plan for love has always been redemptive: joy born from faithfulness, peace born from perseverance, and beauty born from enduring grace.

CONCLUSION

In this chapter, love moves from fear to joy, from searching to celebration. The bride's midnight pursuit and Solomon's radiant procession reveal that true love is not destroyed by distance or darkness. It endures because it is rooted in covenant faithfulness, not fleeting emotion. Every relationship faces nights of uncertainty, but steadfast devotion transforms them into dawns of renewed trust. The bride's joy at reunion and the crown of gladness at the wedding remind us that love's greatest triumph is not passion's height but faith's endurance. In every home where devotion endures through hardship, God's light breaks the night once again.

REFLECTION

1. What emotions and fears surface in the bride's search through the night?

2. How does her perseverance reveal the nature of covenant love?

3. Why is the setting of the "mother's house" important to understanding godly intimacy?

4. What lessons can modern believers learn from the refrain about waiting for love's proper time?

5. How do Solomon's guards symbolize the need to protect relationships from harm?

6. In what ways does this chapter move from fear to joy, and what does that say about love's strength?

DISCUSSION

1. What kinds of "night seasons" challenge love and faith today?

2. How can couples and friends seek one another faithfully during times of distance or conflict?

3. What practical steps help keep intimacy pure and centered in covenant commitment?

4. What does it mean to "guard love" in a Christian home or marriage?

5. How can the church model both truth and tenderness in addressing love and sexuality?

6. What does the joy of the wedding procession teach believers about God's design for marriage?

4

A MAN ENRAPTURED
SONG OF SONGS 4:1–5:1

Objective: To honor marital intimacy as a sacred gift reflecting God's design, delight, and covenant faithfulness.

INTRODUCTION

A husband once said that every time he saw his wife walking toward him, even after decades of marriage, his heart still "skipped like a record." He wasn't speaking of infatuation but of awe—the kind that comes from loving someone deeply and faithfully over time. His words could have been spoken by the man in Song of Songs 4.

This chapter captures a moment of holy admiration. The groom looks upon his bride and praises her beauty in language that is poetic, pure, and passionate. His words are reverent, not reckless. They remind us that God designed physical affection to be good, not shameful. In this scene, love's desire is expressed through devotion, purity, and joy. The man's enraptured heart and the bride's joyful response reveal that passion, when guided by covenant faithfulness, reflects the Creator's own delight in what he has made.

EXAMINATION

The beauty of love described (4:1–7)

The fourth chapter opens with one of Scripture's most tender portraits of marital admiration. The groom speaks first: "Behold, you are beautiful, my love; behold, you are beautiful." Twice he repeats the phrase, as if overwhelmed by what he sees. His tone is not that of possession but of wonder. In these verses we hear the voice of a man enraptured—not by lust, but by love that delights in its beloved.

Scholars describe this section as a *wasf*, an ancient Near Eastern "song of description," in which lovers praise one another's physical beauty. In Hebrew poetry, this form celebrates not the objectification of the body but the reverence of it. The body is seen as part of God's good creation, deserving to be admired within covenant affection.

The groom begins with her eyes—"Your eyes are doves behind your veil." The dove evokes peace, gentleness, and purity. Her gaze is tender yet mysterious, hidden "behind the veil." The veil conceals and reveals at once, heightening anticipation and honoring modesty. Love's mystery is not a barrier to intimacy; it is its invitation.

He moves downward, describing her hair "like a flock of goats leaping down the slopes of Gilead." To the modern ear this sounds odd, but in its setting the image is vivid and beautiful. The dark, flowing locks of the bride resemble a shimmering herd descending the green hillsides of Gilead. In his eyes, her movement captivates him like the living rhythm of creation itself.

Her teeth "are like a flock of shorn ewes that have come up from the washing, all of them bearing twins, not one among them has lost its young." In an age without dental care, white, even, complete teeth were rare and praiseworthy. His delight is both affectionate and playful—his words celebrate her vitality and youth.

He continues: "Your lips are like a scarlet thread, and your mouth is lovely." The deep red color suggests vitality, warmth, and the sweetness of speech. "Your cheeks are like halves of a pomegranate behind your veil," perhaps describing a healthy, glowing complexion. In the ancient world, the pomegranate was a symbol of fertility and beauty; its rich color and abundant seeds made it a fitting image for life and love.

"Your neck is like the tower of David, built in rows of stone; on it hang a thousand shields." Modern readers might imagine rigidity, but this image conveys strength, dignity, and poise. Her bearing is regal, not haughty. Love sees the beloved as noble and steadfast. The shields adorning the tower may hint at necklaces or ornaments that enhance her beauty. She stands with confidence—strong, yet graceful.

Finally, he praises her breasts: "Your two breasts are like two fawns, twins of a gazelle, that graze among the lilies." The imagery conveys gentleness and innocence rather than indulgence. The fawns evoke natural beauty and tender vulnerability. His admiration is reverent, not crude. These verses affirm that Scripture does not blush at physical love when it is sanctified by covenant. Desire in marriage is not sinful; it is sacred.

The man's praise concludes, "Until the day breathes and the shadows flee, I will go away to the mountain of myrrh and the hill of frankincense." The fragrant language points toward the sweetness of union, suggesting both longing and fulfillment. The final verse declares, "You are altogether beautiful, my love; there is no flaw in you." This is not hyperbole—it is the language of adoration. Love chooses to see the beloved through the eyes of grace.

The call of invitation (4:8–15)

The scene shifts from description to invitation. The man's voice beckons: "Come with me from Lebanon, my bride; come with me from Lebanon." He calls her away from the wild, dangerous mountains—"from the dens of lions, from the mountains of leopards"—into the safety of his embrace. The distance between them symbolizes separation, and his words invite union. Love that is secure creates a place of peace where fear cannot dwell.

For the first time, he calls her "my bride." The word marks a turning point in the Song. Their love is no longer merely longing—it is covenantal. The repetition of "my sister, my bride" throughout this section expresses intimacy with purity. In the ancient Near East, "sister" was a term of deep affection and equality. It conveyed companionship and mutual care. Their relationship is not built on domination but on shared devotion.

He continues, "You have captivated my heart, my sister, my bride; you have captivated my heart with one glance of your eyes, with one jewel of your necklace." The Hebrew literally says, "You have made my heart beat faster." His passion is stirred not by possession but by admiration. A single look disarms him. Love that is godly does not seek to control; it rejoices in being undone by wonder.

His praise grows richer: "How beautiful is your love, my sister, my bride! How much better is your love than wine, and the fragrance of your oils than any spice!" Love is not just seen or felt—it is savored. Her affection, her presence, her scent—all are sweeter than life's finest pleasures.

The imagery deepens: "Your lips drip nectar, my bride; honey and milk are under your tongue." The language of taste evokes delight and intimacy, reminiscent of the promised land "flowing with milk and honey." The joy of covenant love is both physical and spiritual—abundance shared between equals.

Then comes one of the most profound metaphors in the Song: "A garden locked is my sister, my bride, a spring locked, a fountain sealed." The locked garden symbolizes both purity and exclusivity. Her love is not available to all—it is preserved for the one to whom she has given her heart. In the ancient world, a sealed fountain was precious; its waters were pure because they were protected. So too, marital intimacy is beautiful precisely because it is private and guarded by faithfulness.

Her garden bursts with abundance: "Your shoots are an orchard of pomegranates with all choicest fruits, henna with nard, nard and saffron, calamus and cinnamon, with every kind of incense tree, myrrh and aloes, with all choice spices." This vivid catalog of scents and spices portrays her as life-giving and desirable—a paradise of delight. In Hebrew thought, the garden evokes Eden restored. The lovers' joy in one another echoes humanity's original harmony in creation.

The man's imagery also highlights the mutuality of their love. She is not an object to be consumed but a living garden that responds. His admiration invites, not invades. Their intimacy is the fruit of trust and tenderness. The sacredness of marriage lies not in secrecy but in the self-giving joy of two hearts joined before God.

The joy of consummation (4:16–5:1)

The woman now speaks for the first time in this sequence, and her words transform the poem from admiration to invitation: "Awake, O north wind, and come, O south wind! Blow upon my garden; let its spices flow." The winds—north and south, cool and warm—symbolize the full range of love's delight. She invites her beloved to enter her garden and share its fruit. The imagery is bold yet pure, celebrating mutual desire within covenant trust.

This moment, often called the climax of the Song, portrays the holiness of marital union. It is not voyeuristic or crude; it is worshipful in tone. She calls her beloved to "come into his garden," acknowledging that what was once hers alone is now theirs together. The language of possession has become language of communion and consummation.

The man answers: "I have come into my garden, my sister, my bride; I have gathered my myrrh with my spice, I have eaten my honeycomb with my honey, I have drunk my wine with my milk." What was anticipated has now been realized. Their love, once restrained by waiting, is now complete in covenant joy.

Then the chorus—perhaps the "friends" or "daughters of Jerusalem"—calls out: "Eat, friends; drink, and be drunk with love." This benediction is stunning. Scripture rarely celebrates physical love so openly, but here it blesses it without apology. Marital intimacy, when holy and faithful, is an act of divine delight. It mirrors the joy of Eden before the fall, when man and woman were naked and unashamed.

The theology of delight

Song of Songs 4:1–5:1 presents a vision of love that is neither prudish nor permissive. It sanctifies passion within the bounds of purity. The lovers' joy is not the reckless ecstasy of lust but the reverent joy of covenant. Desire, in this vision, is not an enemy of holiness but its companion when governed by faithfulness.

This passage also teaches that admiration within marriage is a form of worship. The groom's words—delighting in every detail of his bride—reflect the Creator's own delight in his creation. When love is expressed with tenderness, gratitude, and fidelity, it becomes a testimony of divine goodness.

At the same time, the Song reminds believers that intimacy flourishes only in mutual respect and restraint. The "locked garden" teaches that love must be exclusive, and the refrain throughout the Song—"Do not awaken love until it pleases"—remains wisdom for every generation. Love awakened too soon is fragile; love tended in patience is eternal.

Ultimately, the consummation scene points beyond marriage to the joy of union that all believers will one day know with God himself—a relationship of perfect intimacy, unbroken trust, and everlasting delight. In that sense, the garden of the Song becomes a glimpse of the paradise we were made for: a world where love, pure and strong, is the crown of creation.

APPLICATION

1. God designed physical desire to be holy within covenant love

This chapter celebrates passion not as sin but as sacred. In a world that distorts intimacy through lust, selfishness, or shame, the Song restores its dignity. The groom's admiration and the bride's openness show that desire and devotion can coexist. When God's boundaries are honored, physical affection becomes an expression of trust, not exploitation. Christian marriages should not fear passion but redeem it—keeping it grounded in covenant faithfulness. Every act of tenderness between husband and wife is meant to reflect the Creator's joy in his creation. When believers treat desire as God's gift rather than the world's toy, love becomes both pure and powerful.

2. Words of admiration nurture emotional and spiritual intimacy

The groom's lavish praise reveals that love thrives on affirmation. He names every feature of his bride with care, dignity, and delight. His words do not flatter; they honor. Many relationships suffer not from lack of love but from lack of expression. The Song teaches Christians that verbal affection is holy speech. When a husband and wife continually speak encouragement and admiration, they echo the voice of God, who delights in his people. Our words have the power to build or to break, to bless or to wound. A loving tongue strengthens the covenant bond and rekindles warmth even in weary seasons. Speaking beauty is a form of faithfulness—it reminds both giver and receiver of the goodness of God's design.

3. Purity protects the joy of intimacy

The "garden locked" and "fountain sealed" stand as enduring symbols of faithfulness. The bride's exclusivity is not repression but reverence. Her purity preserves the beauty of their union and magnifies its joy. In the same way, Christians protect intimacy through moral and emotional boundaries that honor God. Premarital restraint and marital fidelity are not outdated virtues—they are the walls that guard Eden. When Christians treat their bodies and hearts as sacred trusts, they safeguard what God intends to be beautiful. Purity is not the absence of desire; it is the discipline that keeps desire holy. True joy in marriage arises when both partners know that their love is unshared, unspoiled, and secure.

4. Covenant intimacy mirrors divine delight

When the lovers rejoice in their union, the chorus blesses them: "Eat, friends; drink, and be drunk with love." That blessing signals heaven's approval. God delights in the joy of his people when they live according to his design. Marital intimacy, far from being taboo, becomes a testimony of divine goodness. It foreshadows the eternal communion between Christ and the church—a relationship marked by joy, trust, and delight. Every faithful marriage therefore becomes a living parable of grace. When husbands and wives love sacrificially, delight mutually, and forgive readily, they reveal the character of the God who rejoices over his people with singing. Love's highest goal is not pleasure but glory—the reflection of divine joy in human covenant.

CONCLUSION

Song of Songs 4:1–5:1 celebrates love at its holiest—where passion and purity unite under covenant faithfulness. The man's praise and the woman's invitation reveal that God's design for intimacy is not to be feared but cherished. Their joy is not selfish indulgence but self-giving delight, echoing the Creator's own pleasure in what is good. In a world that distorts love into either shame or excess, this passage restores its sacred balance. When Christians honor marriage as God intended—exclusive, tender, and joyful—they reflect his faithfulness and glory. Every act of love rooted in covenant grace becomes a small echo of Eden restored.

REFLECTION

1. What do the groom's words reveal about how God views physical love within marriage?

2. How does the "locked garden" image reshape your understanding of purity and protection?

3. Why does the man's admiration of his bride reflect God's delight in his creation?

4. What can we learn about the importance of verbal affirmation in marriage?

5. How does this passage balance passion with restraint, desire with devotion?

6. What glimpses of divine joy appear in the closing blessing, "Eat, friends; drink, and be drunk with love"?

DISCUSSION

1. How can Christian couples cultivate admiration and tenderness over time?

2. What are some modern "foxes" that threaten purity and trust in relationships today?

3. Why is it important for churches to teach both holiness and joy in marriage?

4. How can believers help one another uphold sexual integrity in a culture of indulgence?

5. What practical steps strengthen emotional and spiritual intimacy between spouses?

6. In what ways does covenant love in marriage reflect the gospel of Christ and his church?

5

THE LOVERS ENTRANCED

SONG OF SONGS 5:2–6:10

Objective: To embrace love's maturity through pursuit, remembrance, forgiveness, and renewal in covenant faithfulness.

INTRODUCTION

A married couple once shared how they nearly gave up. "We loved each other," the wife said, "but somewhere along the way, we forgot how to see each other." They spent months living in quiet frustration—until one evening, they sat down and began listing everything they still admired about one another. By the time they finished, they were holding hands again. "Nothing had changed," the husband said, "except that we remembered."

That moment captures the heart of Song of Songs 5–6. The lovers who once rejoiced in union now find themselves separated by misunderstanding and delay. Yet their story does not end in distance—it moves toward renewal. Through longing, memory, and forgiveness, their love matures. The bride learns to seek again; the groom learns to praise again. Together they rediscover that real love is not fragile—it endures, heals, and rejoices anew.

EXAMINATION

Love disturbed and delayed (5:2-8)

The fourth scene of the Song shifts abruptly from the joy of consummation to the tension of absence. "I slept, but my heart was awake. A sound! My beloved is knocking." The contrast between physical rest and inner restlessness captures the experience of every marriage—moments when closeness gives way to distance, when love must learn endurance. The bride dreams of her beloved seeking entrance: "Open to me, my sister, my love, my dove, my perfect one." His words are tender, even urgent. He speaks of being "wet with dew," a poetic sign that he has come through the night to reach her.

Her response, however, reveals hesitation: "I had put off my garment; how could I put it on? I had bathed my feet; how could I soil them?" In her dream, she delays, perhaps out of weariness, complacency, or even fear. The delay is not rebellion but the hesitancy that sometimes cools affection after intimacy. By the time she rises and opens the door, he is gone: "My beloved had turned and gone; my soul failed me when he spoke."

The dream continues with vivid emotion. She searches through the night as before (echoing 3:1-4), but this time the watchmen find her—and wound her. "They struck me, they bruised me; they took away my veil." The imagery is not literal violence but symbolic pain—the anguish of separation and misunderstanding. The bride's vulnerability is exposed. The veil once representing intimacy now becomes the mark of her sorrow.

This dream sequence reflects the recurring rhythms of love—longing, frustration, renewal. Even the strongest marriages face moments when affection seems distant and communication falters. Yet longing can become a teacher; the ache of absence deepens appreciation for presence. The bride's cry to the "daughters of Jerusalem" at the end of the dream—"If you find my beloved, tell him I am sick with love"—turns pain into prayer. Her heart, though wounded, still yearns. True love does not die in disappointment; it longs for reconciliation.

Love remembered and praised (5:9-6:3)

The chorus of young women responds, "What is your beloved more than another beloved, O most beautiful among women?" Their question invites the bride to describe her husband, and in doing so, she rekindles her affection. Memory becomes medicine. Her words pour out in a *wasf*—a poetic description of his beauty, matching his earlier praise of her in chapter 4. Love that was wounded begins to heal through remembrance.

She begins: "My beloved is radiant and ruddy, distinguished among ten thousand." The two colors—white and red—symbolize purity and strength. He is both gentle and courageous, graceful and powerful. "His head is the finest gold; his locks are wavy, black as a raven." The precious metal conveys honor and nobility; the dark hair, vigor and youth. Her admiration is total—she sees no flaw in him.

"His eyes are like doves beside streams of water, bathed in milk, sitting beside a full pool." The imagery recalls calmness and clarity; his eyes reflect peace and compassion. "His cheeks are like beds of spices, mounds of sweet-smelling herbs. His lips are lilies, dripping liquid myrrh." Each detail evokes fragrance and sweetness—the senses of smell and taste join sight and sound to paint a portrait of deep affection.

She continues: "His arms are rods of gold, set with jewels. His body is polished ivory, bedecked with sapphires. His legs are alabaster columns, set on bases of gold." The imagery moves from head to foot, echoing the pattern of the earlier descriptions of her. Her praise builds to the final declaration: "His mouth is most sweet, and he is altogether desirable. This is my beloved, and this is my friend."

That last line is the crown of the description. Love matures when passion becomes friendship. Desire alone cannot sustain a marriage, but friendship gives it endurance. The bride's recollection of her beloved rekindles both her affection and her peace. Memory transforms absence into renewal.

The chorus replies again in 6:1: "Where has your beloved gone, O most beautiful among women? Where has your beloved turned, that we may seek him with you?" The community now joins her in the search. Love that once felt private now invites fellowship and accountability. Relationships strengthened by godly community often find restoration faster than those isolated by pride.

The bride answers in 6:2–3 with confidence and calm: "My beloved has gone down to his garden, to the beds of spices, to graze in the gardens and to gather lilies. I am my beloved's and my beloved is mine; he grazes among the lilies." The imagery of the garden returns—a symbol of intimacy restored. The phrase "I am my beloved's and my beloved is mine" is the mature form of covenant belonging. Earlier in 2:16 she said, "My beloved is mine, and I am his." The order has now reversed. She begins with surrender: "I am my beloved's." Maturity in love means moving from possession to devotion, from claiming to yielding.

Love renewed and restored (6:4–10)

The final section of this scene presents reconciliation and renewed affection. The man speaks again, his tone full of admiration: "You are beautiful as Tirzah, my love, lovely as Jerusalem, awesome as an army with banners." Tirzah and Jerusalem were the two most splendid cities of ancient Israel—symbols of majesty and harmony. By comparing her to them, he elevates her dignity and worth. She is not only beautiful to him; she is magnificent.

"Turn away your eyes from me, for they overwhelm me." The word literally means "to terrify" or "to unsettle." Her gaze disarms him. The very sight of her rekindles desire and reverence. Love that has survived separation now burns brighter for having endured it.

The familiar imagery of chapter 4 returns, but with subtle variation. "Your hair is like a flock of goats leaping down the slopes of Gilead. Your teeth are like a flock of ewes that have come up from the washing, all of them bearing twins." The repetition suggests continuity—their affection is renewed, not replaced. "Your cheeks are like halves of a pomegranate behind your veil." The same features he once praised now reappear, but the tone has deepened. The bride who was once sought is now secure.

He continues, "There are sixty queens and eighty concubines, and virgins without number. My dove, my perfect one, is the only one." His praise emphasizes exclusivity. Even amid abundance, she alone satisfies him. This statement carries moral weight: true love is not distracted by novelty. Fidelity is the beauty of the soul that refuses comparison. In a world where desire is divided, devotion remains whole.

The chorus echoes the man's admiration in 6:10, describing the woman's radiance: "Who is this who looks down like the dawn, beautiful as the moon, bright as the sun, awesome as an army with banners?" The imagery now mirrors his earlier praise, showing that their love, once private, now commands public honor. The dawn dispels the night; light triumphs over darkness. What began as a dream of distance ends with restoration and rejoicing.

The theology of reconciliation

Song of Songs 5:2–6:10 is a masterpiece of emotional realism. It portrays not idealized lovers immune to struggle, but real love that endures conflict and emerges stronger. The alternating scenes of absence, memory, and reunion mirror the natural seasons of marriage—moments of misunderstanding followed by renewal.

Theologically, this passage reveals that love's strength lies not in avoiding pain but in persevering through it. The bride's search, though painful, leads to rediscovery. Her wounded heart becomes the soil where deeper devotion grows. The groom's renewed admiration shows grace in action: he does not reproach her for delay but restores her with praise.

The refrain "I am my beloved's and my beloved is mine" becomes a confession of covenant grace. Theirs is not a perfect love, but a persevering one—reflecting God's steadfast love that forgives, restores, and rejoices. In marriage, as in faith, renewal often follows repentance.

The lovers' story thus speaks to every Christian marriage: passion must be paired with patience, and affection must be grounded in forgiveness. The God who designed love also redeems it. When love falters, his grace rekindles it; when distance grows, his wisdom restores it. Every act of reconciliation between husband and wife becomes a small reflection of the greater reconciliation between God and his people—the love that endures even through the night and greets the dawn with joy.

APPLICATION

1. Love matures through seasons of distance and renewal

The bride's dream of separation teaches that even the strongest marriages experience times of emotional distance. Affection can fade when fatigue, pride, or distraction enter. Yet absence is not the end—it becomes an invitation to deeper pursuit. Godly love learns to seek again. When couples face silence or misunderstanding, they can respond either with resentment or renewal. The bride's persistence shows the right path: she rises to search, refusing to surrender her love to discouragement. In every marriage, God uses seasons of struggle to refine devotion. The ache of longing reminds believers that love must be tended, not taken for granted.

2. Remembering the good rekindles affection

When asked to describe her beloved, the bride recalls his virtues with vivid joy. Her words heal what distance wounded. Memory becomes the medicine of reconciliation. In times of disappointment, it is easy to fixate on faults; the Song calls us instead to remember the gifts. Marriages thrive when spouses choose gratitude over grumbling. Reflecting on the other's goodness softens the heart and renews affection. For Christians, this practice mirrors worship itself—remembering what God has done restores faith. In the same way, remembering why we fell in love restores tenderness. Love's memory guards the heart from bitterness and keeps admiration alive through every season.

3. Faithful devotion is stronger than comparison

When the man praises his bride as "the only one," he contrasts her purity and faithfulness with the multitude of others who might seek his attention. In a world that prizes novelty, Scripture exalts loyalty. True love refuses comparison. It is content with the one God has given. Temptation often begins not with desire but with discontent—the quiet belief that something else would be better. But covenant love rejects that lie. Devotion flourishes when the heart stops looking elsewhere and starts rejoicing in the beloved's worth. A Christian marriage guarded by faithfulness becomes a refuge of peace in a restless world.

4. Reconciliation reveals the heart of divine love

The lovers' reunion after separation reflects the redemptive nature of love itself. Their story moves from absence to presence, from longing to joy. Likewise, the gospel is the story of reconciliation—God seeking those who have wandered and restoring them through grace. When husbands and wives forgive, they enact the gospel in miniature. Love that endures offense testifies to a greater mercy at work. Every apology offered, every gentle word spoken after conflict, becomes holy ground where grace triumphs over pride. The joy of reunion in this chapter points beyond human affection to divine compassion—the love that never lets go, even when wounded.

CONCLUSION

This passage reminds Christians that love's strength is proven not in perfection but in perseverance. The lovers face distance, misunderstanding, and heartache, yet their devotion endures. Through longing, remembrance, and reconciliation, their affection deepens and matures. The refrain "I am my beloved's and my beloved is mine" becomes the heartbeat of covenant faithfulness—a love refined by grace. Every Christian marriage will experience its nights of silence and its mornings of renewal. What matters is the willingness to seek, to forgive, and to remember. When love chooses restoration over resentment, it reflects the very heart of God, whose steadfast love never ceases and whose mercies are new every morning.

REFLECTION

1. What does the bride's dream teach us about the emotional rhythms of love and marriage?

2. How does longing in absence deepen rather than diminish true affection?

3. Why is remembering the good such a powerful tool for healing relational distance?

4. What does the phrase "I am my beloved's and my beloved is mine" reveal about mature love?

5. How does faithfulness bring security and peace in a relationship?

6. What glimpses of God's own steadfast love appear in the couple's reconciliation?

DISCUSSION

1. What are practical ways couples can pursue each other again after seasons of distance?

2. How can Christians use gratitude and memory to strengthen their marriages?

3. In what ways does Christian faith reshape how we handle conflict and reconciliation?

4. What makes exclusivity and loyalty such vital parts of covenant love?

5. How does this chapter's portrayal of forgiveness mirror the gospel itself?

6. What lessons from the lovers' reunion can help modern Christians cultivate enduring joy?

6

THE DANCE OF DELIGHTS

SONG OF SONGS 6:11–7:13

Objective: To celebrate mature love that delights, endures, and reflects God's joy through mutual devotion and faithfulness.

INTRODUCTION

At a wedding anniversary dinner, a husband stood to toast his wife. With a grin he said, "After all these years, she still makes my heart race—though now it might be the cholesterol." Laughter filled the room, but then his voice softened. "Truth is," he continued, "we've learned to love not just with our hearts, but with our history."

That spirit defines this section of the Song of Songs. The lovers, once separated by misunderstanding, now rejoice together in renewed affection. Their words are tender but confident, filled with admiration and delight. What began as youthful passion has matured into joyful companionship. Through poetic imagery of gardens, fragrance, and dance, the Song celebrates love that lasts—and love that laughs. This is the beauty of covenant affection: passion preserved by purity, joy deepened by faithfulness, and delight restored by grace.

EXAMINATION

The garden revisited (6:11-13)

After reconciliation and renewed affection, the Song moves into a scene of joy and celebration. The bride speaks first: "I went down to the nut orchard to look at the blossoms of the valley, to see whether the vines had budded, whether the pomegranates were in bloom." Her words echo the imagery of springtime from earlier in the Song (2:10-13). Love, once wounded, now flourishes again. The garden, a recurring symbol of intimacy, has come back to life.

The "nut orchard" (literally, "garden of nuts") reflects abundance and renewal. The bride goes to survey what has grown—to see if love's fruit has returned after a season of distance. She finds not barrenness but beauty. Her visit to the garden represents more than curiosity; it signifies reconciliation verified by experience. Love has endured, and its blossoms testify to grace.

Then comes an enigmatic verse: "Before I was aware, my desire set me among the chariots of my kinsman, a prince" (6:12). The meaning is uncertain, but the poetry is clear—she is swept up in a sudden rush of emotion. The Hebrew word translated "desire" (or "soul") conveys deep yearning. In an instant, she is carried away in joy and exhilaration, perhaps imagining herself restored to the full delight of her beloved. Some interpreters see the "chariots" as a metaphor for passion's power—love moves swiftly and irresistibly, like a royal procession.

The next verse shifts perspective. "Return, return, O Shulammite; return, return, that we may look upon you." The chorus of onlookers—likely the "daughters of Jerusalem"—calls to the bride, urging her to reappear. The repetition of "return" conveys excitement and admiration. The name "Shulammite" (used only here in Scripture) likely means "the peaceful one" or "the woman from Shulem," a feminine form of "Solomon." The pairing of their names—Solomon and the Shulammite—symbolizes perfect harmony. She mirrors him as his counterpart, his equal in affection and honor.

The onlookers ask, "Why should you look upon the Shulammite, as upon a dance before two armies?" The phrase "dance before two armies" (or "dance of Mahanaim") evokes both beauty and awe. The bride becomes the focus of celebration, her grace commanding the attention of all. The tension of earlier chapters has dissolved into joy. Love, once threatened, now triumphs openly, as though all creation joins the dance.

The beauty of the beloved (7:1–9)

The next section continues the celebratory tone but shifts the speaker. The man now describes his bride in another *wasf*—a poetic song of physical admiration. This description, one of the most detailed in the Song, begins from the ground up, reversing the order of his earlier praise in chapter 4. The reversal may symbolize that their relationship has deepened—from the heights of infatuation to the steady foundation of mature affection.

"How beautiful are your feet in sandals, O noble daughter! Your rounded thighs are like jewels, the work of a master hand." The man begins with her feet, perhaps as she dances before him. Sandals were symbols of both freedom and dignity. To call her a "noble daughter" honors her character as much as her form. His praise affirms her dignity; she is beautiful and honorable, graceful and good.

"Your navel is a rounded bowl that never lacks mixed wine. Your belly is a heap of wheat, encircled with lilies." These metaphors strike modern readers as strange, but in their context, they express admiration for life, nourishment, and fertility. The bride's body symbolizes abundance—the place from which life and joy flow. Wheat and wine were Israel's chief blessings of harvest; here they stand for satisfaction and delight.

He continues upward: "Your two breasts are like two fawns, twins of a gazelle." The image repeats from 4:5, suggesting enduring affection. What once symbolized anticipation now signifies fulfillment and faithfulness. The constancy of this image mirrors the constancy of his love.

"Your neck is like an ivory tower. Your eyes are pools in Heshbon, by the gate of Bath-rabbim. Your nose is like a tower of Lebanon, which looks toward Damascus." Each metaphor joins beauty with strength. Ivory and towers suggest purity, elegance, and dignity. Her eyes, deep and clear, reflect calm confidence. Her "nose," far from a critique, represents noble profile—a sign of character and countenance. The poet celebrates not vanity but vitality. Every feature becomes an emblem of her moral and spiritual grace.

"Your head crowns you like Carmel, and your flowing locks are like purple; a king is held captive in the tresses." Mount Carmel, lush and majestic, symbolizes fertility and grandeur. Her hair, described as royal purple, radiates allure. Yet even here, the tone remains reverent. The phrase "a king is held captive" does not suggest domination but fascination. Love's power is mutual—the husband is willingly conquered by his wife's beauty, just as she earlier was enraptured by his voice. Mutual admiration, not control, defines covenant love.

He sums up his delight in 7:6–9: "How beautiful and pleasant you are, O loved one, with all your delights! Your stature is like a palm tree, and your breasts are like its clusters. I say I will climb the palm tree and lay hold of its fruit. Oh may your breasts be like clusters of the vine, and the scent of your breath like apples, and your mouth like the best wine." The imagery grows increasingly intimate, yet it remains poetic and dignified. The palm tree, upright and fruitful, was a symbol of beauty and life in the ancient world. To "climb the palm tree" and "take hold of its fruit" expresses desire for closeness, not exploitation. The language conveys delight that is mutual, not one-sided; his passion is framed by admiration and covenant loyalty.

At the end of verse 9, her voice gently overlaps his: "It goes down smoothly for my beloved, gliding over lips and teeth." The shift of voice illustrates unity—they speak as one. Love's harmony is restored. Their conversation moves seamlessly between admiration and participation, a verbal dance mirroring the physical one.

The response of love (7:10–13)

The bride responds with confidence and invitation. "I am my beloved's, and his desire is for me." This declaration reverses the disorder introduced in Genesis 3:16, where sin distorted desire into domination. In the Song, redemption restores balance—desire is no longer a struggle but a joy. Mutual belonging replaces rivalry. Her words reveal contentment, not dependence; love has matured into trust.

"Come, my beloved, let us go out into the fields and lodge in the villages; let us go out early to the vineyards and see whether the vines have budded, whether the grape blossoms have opened and the pomegranates are in bloom." The imagery recalls their early courtship in chapter 2, but now the setting is pastoral peace, not anxious pursuit. Love that began in passion now abides in companionship. Their shared labor and leisure show that marital affection encompasses daily life.

"There I will give you my love." This phrase, simple yet profound, sanctifies intimacy as worshipful. Their union is neither secretive nor shameful; it is the culmination of covenant devotion. She continues: "The mandrakes give forth fragrance, and beside our doors are all choice fruits, new as well as old, which I have laid up for you, O my beloved." The mandrake, an ancient symbol of fertility, enhances the scene's sense of abundance. The "choice fruits, new and old" represent both the freshness and endurance of love—affections that are renewed daily yet enriched by history.

The theology of delight

This passage brings the Song to its height of joy and maturity. The lovers' journey from longing to fulfillment mirrors the spiritual rhythm of faith itself—desire, pursuit, renewal, and delight. In this section, the body and soul unite in harmony; passion serves fidelity, and pleasure glorifies God. The sensual imagery, when read within its covenant context, celebrates the holiness of embodied love.

Theologically, this chapter teaches that joy and holiness are not opposites but allies. God is not embarrassed by human affection; he designed it to reflect his own joy in creation. The husband's admiration and the wife's confident response show that covenant love thrives in mutual honor and delight. When expressed with purity and faithfulness, physical love becomes a form of praise—a reminder that the Creator who made bodies also blesses their union.

The bride's closing invitation—"Come, my beloved"—recalls the divine call echoed throughout Scripture. The intimacy of marriage foreshadows the deeper communion believers share with God himself. In both relationships, love is not static; it moves, dances, delights. As the Shulammite rejoices in her beloved, so the faithful soul rejoices in the Lord who rejoices over his people with singing (Zeph. 3:17).

APPLICATION

1. Enduring love become rejoicing love

The Shulammite's journey to the garden shows that love tested by time becomes stronger and sweeter. Seasons of distance and renewal give way to delight. Mature love doesn't live on passion alone—it learns to dance again after hardship. When a husband and wife choose joy after disappointment, they proclaim that grace has triumphed. God intends marriage to echo this rhythm: sorrow turned to laughter, separation turned to song. The "dance of delights" is not naïve happiness; it is the joy of two souls who have weathered the storms together. Christian couples can celebrate not just the beauty of new love, but the blessing of love that endures.

2. Admiration is a language of covenant grace

The groom's song of praise demonstrates that admiration is not vanity—it is devotion expressed in words. He names his bride's beauty with reverence and delight, honoring her dignity as one made in God's image. Words of affirmation strengthen love because they remind both giver and receiver that affection is a choice, not a mere feeling. Silence starves intimacy, but gracious speech nourishes it. In every marriage, the art of admiration must be practiced intentionally. Compliments, gratitude, and tenderness are sacred acts that reflect the Creator's own delight in his creation. When believers speak beauty to one another, they join in the holy language of covenant love.

3. Godly intimacy unites pleasure and purity

The imagery of this chapter celebrates physical love without shame because it rests within covenant faithfulness. In a culture that distorts sexuality, the Song restores its sacredness. The husband's desire and the wife's invitation are pure because they are mutual, faithful, and joyful. God designed the body as an instrument of affection, not exploitation. True intimacy, grounded in trust and exclusivity, mirrors divine love—it gives, honors, and delights. Christian couples should see physical closeness as a gift to nurture, not a duty to perform. In loving one another tenderly and faithfully, they reflect the holiness of the God who rejoices in his good creation.

4. Love's renewal reflects the joy of redemption

When the bride declares, "I am my beloved's, and his desire is for me," she speaks the language of restoration. Once marked by distance and doubt, her relationship now radiates peace and belonging. That transformation mirrors the gospel. God's love does not discard the broken; it renews them. Every reconciliation in marriage becomes a living testimony of divine grace. The same God who redeems sinners also revives weary hearts. In Christ, forgiveness always leads to joy. The lovers' song teaches believers that renewal is possible—not only in marriage, but in every relationship touched by mercy. Love that forgives becomes love that dances again.

CONCLUSION

The dance of delights shows that love refined by time becomes love renewed by grace. The bride and groom, once separated, now rejoice in harmony—their admiration, affection, and intimacy restored. Scripture presents their joy not as indulgence but as worship: the celebration of God's good design for love within covenant faithfulness. In their laughter and longing, we glimpse the Creator's own joy in his people. Christian marriages flourish when couples nurture both tenderness and trust, keeping affection alive through grace and gratitude. Love that delights after hardship reveals a deeper beauty—the beauty of redemption, where faithfulness and joy meet once again in the garden of God's design.

REFLECTION

1. What does the Shulammite's return to the garden symbolize about love's renewal?

2. How does admiration strengthen the bond between husband and wife?

3. Why is it important that physical love is celebrated within covenant commitment?

4. What does it mean for joy to follow after seasons of struggle or distance?

5. How do the husband's words reveal the beauty of mutual respect and delight?

6. What parallels exist between the lovers' restoration and God's redemptive love?

DISCUSSION

1. How can couples learn to celebrate one another's worth through both words and actions?

2. What habits or choices help keep affection alive in long-term relationships?

3. In what ways can the church teach a positive, biblical view of intimacy and desire?

4. Why is mutual admiration a reflection of spiritual maturity in marriage?

5. How does this passage challenge modern ideas about beauty, passion, and commitment?

6. What can the lovers' "dance of delights" teach us about God's joy in his people?

7

LOVE STRONG AS DEATH

SONG OF SONGS 6:11–7:13

Objective: To exalt covenant love as God's enduring flame—faithful, unquenchable, and stronger than death itself.

INTRODUCTION

In 1940, an elderly couple in France was found holding hands in their final moments after their home had been bombed. They had been married more than fifty years. Neighbors said they did everything together—gardening, walking, praying—and even in death, they remained side by side. Their love, one witness said, "was stronger than fear."

That kind of devotion captures the heart of Song of Songs 8. The lovers have journeyed through desire, separation, and reunion, and now their bond stands unbreakable. The bride declares that love is "strong as death, its passion the very flame of the Lord." This is no fleeting emotion but covenant loyalty that endures every storm. The final chapter gathers all the Song's themes—purity, passion, faithfulness, and joy—into a single truth: love that flows from God's heart cannot be quenched. It burns with holy fire and lasts forever.

EXAMINATION

The desire for abiding love (8:1–4)

The final chapter of the Song opens with longing that has matured through love's many seasons. The bride speaks: "Oh that you were like a brother to me who nursed at my mother's breasts! If I found you outside, I would kiss you, and none would despise me." Her words may seem strange to modern ears, but in the ancient Near East, public displays of affection were acceptable only among family. By wishing her beloved were "like a brother," she expresses a desire for open, unhindered intimacy—love unashamed and constant. She does not seek to redefine their relationship but to deepen its freedom.

Her yearning continues: "I would lead you and bring you into the house of my mother—she who used to teach me." The "mother's house" appeared earlier in 3:4, symbolizing covenant safety and familial blessing. Love, at its ripest, seeks permanence and peace. The bride imagines herself nurturing and sustaining her beloved: "I would give you spiced wine to drink, the juice of my pomegranate." The imagery recalls abundance, fertility, and joy. She no longer yearns for the excitement of pursuit but for the calm of companionship.

Her voice softens with the familiar refrain: "His left hand is under my head, and his right hand embraces me." The verse repeats from 2:6 and 5:2, creating a literary frame around the Song's intimacy. It is both tender and symbolic—love that encircles, protects, and delights. Once again, the refrain follows: "I adjure you, O daughters of Jerusalem, that you not stir up or awaken love until it pleases." This warning, appearing now for the final time, seals the Song's wisdom: true love cannot be forced, manipulated, or hurried. It blossoms only in its God-given time.

The power of covenant love (8:5–7)

The next scene opens with a question from the onlookers: "Who is that coming up from the wilderness, leaning on her beloved?" This image recalls the exodus motif—emerging from wilderness into promise. The bride who once searched anxiously for her lover (3:1–4) now walks beside him in peace. She leans upon him, not in weakness, but in mutual trust. The wilderness behind them represents trial and testing; the rest ahead symbolizes fulfillment.

The bride continues: "Under the apple tree I awakened you. There your mother was in labor with you; there she who bore you was in labor." The apple tree, a recurring symbol of delight and fertility, now becomes the site of remembrance. Love, like life, is born through labor and sustained through faithfulness. The mention of childbirth imagery may suggest the generational continuity of love—family, covenant, and blessing intertwined.

Then comes the Song's most famous declaration, a pinnacle of biblical poetry: "Set me as a seal upon your heart, as a seal upon your arm, for love is strong as death, jealousy is fierce as the grave. Its flashes are flashes of fire, the very flame of the Lord. Many waters cannot quench love, neither can floods drown it. If a man offered for love all the wealth of his house, he would be utterly despised."

The "seal" was a mark of ownership, security, and authenticity. To wear a seal on the heart and arm meant that the bond was both internal (emotional devotion) and external (faithful action). Love, in this sense, becomes a covenantal commitment—exclusive, enduring, and visible.

"Love is strong as death." Death claims all; nothing resists it. Yet here, love stands its equal. The bride declares that true love endures every threat, outlasts every storm, and survives every loss. The parallel phrase, "jealousy is fierce as the grave," does not describe envy but zeal—the passionate, protective faithfulness that guards intimacy from betrayal. Such love burns with divine intensity: "Its flashes are flashes of fire, the very flame of the Lord." This is the only explicit mention of God in the Song, reminding readers that the holiness of love derives from its divine origin. Covenant love, like divine love, is consuming yet life-giving, powerful yet pure.

"Many waters cannot quench love, neither can floods drown it." The image evokes Noah's flood and the Red Sea—waters that overwhelm all but what God preserves. True love, sustained by God, cannot be extinguished by adversity. Wealth cannot purchase it; passion alone cannot sustain it. It is a gift—strong, enduring, priceless.

The protection of young love (8:8–12)

After this climactic hymn, the tone turns reflective. The brothers of the bride speak: "We have a little sister, and she has no breasts. What shall we do for our sister on the day when she is spoken for?" Their concern is protective, not patronizing. They represent the family's role in guarding chastity and preparing young women for covenant love. In ancient culture, brothers often served as guardians of their sisters' honor (see Gen. 34).

They continue, "If she is a wall, we will build on her a battlement of silver, but if she is a door, we will enclose her with boards of cedar." The imagery distinguishes between steadfast virtue (a wall) and open vulnerability (a door). The brothers promise to reward faithfulness and to protect against folly. The moral lesson is clear: love must be built upon integrity and guarded by wisdom long before passion awakens.

The bride responds in verse 10 with confidence: "I was a wall, and my breasts were like towers; then I was in his eyes as one who finds peace." Her words affirm her purity and her readiness. The "wall" stands for strength and self-control; the "towers" symbolize maturity and dignity. Because she preserved herself for covenant love, she now enjoys "peace"—the Hebrew *shalom*, a wordplay on her name, "Shulammite." Love's security and satisfaction flow from moral and spiritual faithfulness.

The final verses (8:11–12) contrast Solomon's wealth with the simplicity of genuine love: "Solomon had a vineyard at Baal-hamon; he let out the vineyard to keepers; each one was to bring for its fruit a thousand pieces of silver. My vineyard, my very own, is before me; you, O Solomon, may have the thousand, and the keepers of the fruit two hundred." The bride distinguishes her personal devotion from commercial exchange. Love cannot be rented, traded, or bought. Her "vineyard"—her body and her heart—belong to her beloved alone. In a world that measures worth by wealth, she insists that love's value is in exclusivity, not extravagance.

The final invitation (8:13–14)

The Song closes as it began—with dialogue between the lovers. The man speaks first: "O you who dwell in the gardens, with companions listening for your voice; let me hear it." His request is intimate and personal. He desires her voice, her presence, her affection. The "gardens" may symbolize her world of relationships, friends, and responsibilities, yet even amid the noise, he longs to hear her song. True love cherishes communication.

The final verse belongs to the bride: "Make haste, my beloved, and be like a gazelle or a young stag on the mountains of spices." These are the same words with which she once described him (2:17). The echo brings the

Song full circle. Love that began in longing ends in joy. Desire remains, but now it is sanctified by covenant and sustained by faithfulness. The "mountains of spices" represent the enduring sweetness of their union.

The theology of covenant love

The closing chapter of the Song of Songs elevates love from emotion to vocation. Throughout the book, desire has been disciplined, passion has been purified, and affection has been anchored in faithfulness. Now, in its final act, the Song reveals that love's ultimate strength lies in covenant—the bond that mirrors God's steadfast love for his people.

The great declaration "love is strong as death" anticipates the gospel. In Christ, divine love confronts death itself and prevails. The "flame of the Lord" that burns in covenant marriage also burns in redemption. Human love, when purified and faithful, becomes a reflection of the divine—jealous, enduring, unquenchable.

For Christians, this passage offers both comfort and challenge. It reminds us that marriage is not merely romance but covenant; not mere affection but faithfulness. Love that lasts requires more than emotion—it requires grace. Yet when love is rooted in God, it becomes as strong as death and as enduring as eternity. The Song ends, not with finality, but with invitation: "Make haste, my beloved." Love's story continues in every generation that honors God's design and rejoices in his gift.

APPLICATION

1. True love seeks permanence, not performance

The bride's longing for public, unhindered affection reflects every believer's desire for love that lasts. She no longer craves excitement or novelty but faithfulness and peace. In marriage, love matures when intimacy deepens beyond attraction into abiding trust. The world measures love by emotion and excitement, but Scripture measures it by endurance. Covenant love endures because it is anchored in promise, not performance. Christians must guard against a culture that glorifies temporary passion while neglecting steadfast devotion. A faithful marriage, lived with tenderness and patience, testifies to the God who never abandons his people. Love that endures quietly through the years proclaims the gospel more powerfully than words.

2. Covenant love reflects divine strength

"Love is strong as death." Those words remind us that genuine love carries divine power. It is fierce, protective, and unquenchable because it comes from God. The same fire that sustains marital faithfulness burns in the heart of the Creator who covenants with his people. When couples commit to lifelong fidelity, they mirror that holy flame—the "very flame of the Lord." Love's endurance is not human achievement but divine grace at work. In a world that treats commitment as optional, believers must embody the strength of covenant love. Each act of loyalty, forgiveness, and perseverance declares that love's power is greater than life's trials. God's love is stronger than death; so too, love grounded in him conquers every storm.

3. Purity prepares the heart for peace

The bride's reflection on her youth and the brothers' desire to protect her purity reveal a timeless truth: integrity before marriage shapes peace within marriage. The imagery of the "wall" and "door" reminds believers that self-control is not repression but preparation. The one who honors God before covenant is able to rejoice within it. Christian parents, churches, and mentors must teach that sexual purity is not a rule to stifle joy but a foundation for lasting joy. God designed holiness to protect the heart from regret and to preserve the beauty of intimacy. The Shulammite's peace—the *shalom* of fulfilled love—comes not by chance but by faithfulness. Purity builds the kind of character that can both give and receive love with confidence.

4. Love is most powerful when it gives, not when it gains

The bride's final contrast between Solomon's wealth and her own "vineyard" declares that love cannot be bought or measured by possessions. In covenant love, self-giving replaces self-seeking. The joy of marriage comes not from what one receives but from what one offers—time, grace, patience, devotion. This truth mirrors the gospel itself: God's love is defined not by what he gained, but by what he gave. Every faithful marriage becomes a living parable of that generosity. When husbands and wives learn to love sacrificially, they proclaim that God's love remains the world's greatest treasure. The wealth of Solomon fades; the flame of the Lord endures forever.

CONCLUSION

The Song ends not with farewell but with fire—the unquenchable flame of covenant love. What began as longing now rests in loyalty; what began as desire now abides in devotion. "Love is strong as death," the bride declares, because its strength comes from God himself. Human affection, when shaped by faithfulness and purity, becomes a reflection of divine love—the love that pursues, protects, and perseveres. The Shulammite's peace, her joy, and her final invitation remind believers that the story of love is ultimately the story of redemption. Every home built on such covenant grace becomes a living witness that God's steadfast love truly endures forever.

REFLECTION

1. What do the bride's opening words reveal about her longing for lasting, unashamed love?

2. How does the image of the "seal upon your heart" describe covenant commitment?

3. Why is love compared to both death and fire in this passage?

4. What does the Shulammite's peace teach about the value of purity and faithfulness?

5. How does the contrast between Solomon's wealth and true love challenge worldly values?

6. Where do you see God's own steadfast love reflected in this chapter?

DISCUSSION

1. How can married couples today cultivate the kind of enduring love described in Song 8?

2. In what ways does covenant commitment strengthen rather than limit love's joy?

3. Why is purity before marriage so vital to peace within it?

4. What practical steps help protect relationships from becoming transactional rather than self-giving?

5. How can Christian marriages testify to God's "flame that cannot be quenched"?

6. What truths from this chapter can guide singles in preparing for godly love and covenant faithfulness?

www.ingramcontent.com/pod-product-compliance
Lightning Source LLC
Chambersburg PA
CBHW052125070526
44586CB00016B/2096